Prophet Muhammad (peace and blessings be upon him) said:

Whoever performs Hajj for the sake of Allah and does not utter any obscene speech or do any evil deed, will go back (free of sin) as his mother bore him.

Hadith | Bukhari and Muslim

One summer afternoon, as my mother sat packing,
I excitedly asked her, "Mama, where are we going?"

"We're going on Hajj", said Mama, "it's Dhul-Hijjah",
"These 10 days are most beloved to Allah."

*Dhul-Hijjah- one of the four Holy Months
in the Islamic Calendar

We carefully pack our belongings, clothes, and ihraam,
With taqwa in our hearts, we travel to Masjid Al-Haram.

Before arriving at the Holy city of Makkah,
We put on our ihraam at the station of Miqaat.

Making our intention for Hajj and Umrah,
We say out loud words of the Talbiyah.

*Hajj At-Tamattu- Hajj performed by Muslims who live outside Saudi Arabia.
Umrah and Hajj are combined.

We perform Tawaf 7 times around the Ka'bah,
And at Maqam Ibrahim we pray 2 raka'at.

Between Safa & Marwa we now perform Sa'ee,
While remembering Hajar and her amazing story.

*Hajar – Prophet Ibrahim alayhis-salam's wife,
Prophet Ismail alayhis-salam's mother

For her tawakkul and sabr, Allah rewarded her,
With miraculous ZamZam, pure gushing water.

We shave our heads or trim our hair to complete our 'Umrah,
Renew Ihram, walk to Mina on the 8th of Dhul-Hijjah.

Here we stay in a stretched-out white tent,
Dhuhr, 'Asr and 'Isha we pray 2 raka'at shortened.

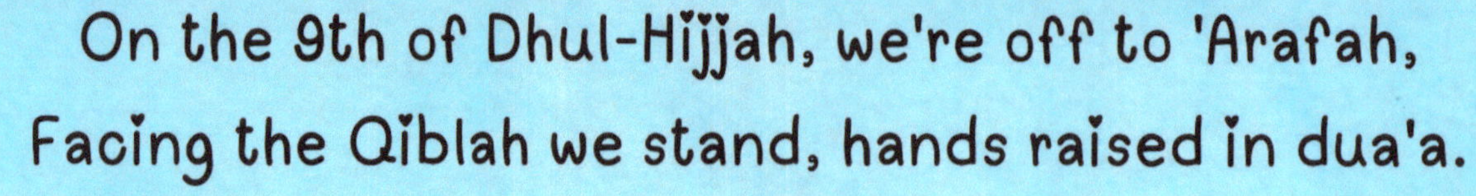

On the 9th of Dhul-Hijjah, we're off to 'Arafah,
Facing the Qiblah we stand, hands raised in dua'a.

I made dua'a for my family and all the muslimeen,
"Ask Allah for Jannah too!" my mother reminded me.

Later we head to Muzdalifah after sunset,
Combine Maghrib and 'Isha, then we rest.

*Rami al-Jamaraat- the act of pelting stones at the three Jamaraat in Mina.
Also known as "Stoning of the Shaytan".

We stone the Large Jamarah one at a time,
Saying "Allahu Akbar" loudly, each time.

Next, we offer Udhiyyah- an animal sacrifice,
And perform Halq/Taqseer following Hajj rites.

*Halq- Shaving the head, for men
Taqseer - Trimming of the hair (by an inch), for women

Now we're out of ihraam, and in our usual clothes,
To perform Tawaf and Sa'ee, back to Makkah we go.

10th,11th & 12th Dhul-Hijjah, in Mina we'll stay,
To stone all 3 Jamaraat, picking 21 stones each day.

On the 13th of Dhul-Hijjah, we return to Makkah,
Circle the Ka'bah one last time for Tawaf al-Wida.

Hajj is a great deed, and a sacred journey,
Allah rewards us with Jannah, when it's done sincerely.

We thank Allah, grateful for all His blessings,
Mama's cooked a delicious feast, I can't wait to dig in!

My first Hajj, I'll cherish it fondly in my heart,
Alhamdulillah, now it's time to celebrate Eid-ul-Adha!

My Hajj Map

MIQAAT
MAKKAH
SA'I
MUZDALIFAH
ARAFAH
AL-MINA
JAMARAH AL-KUBRA
SACRIFICE
TAWAF
FAREWELL TAWAF
RAMI AL-JAMARAAT

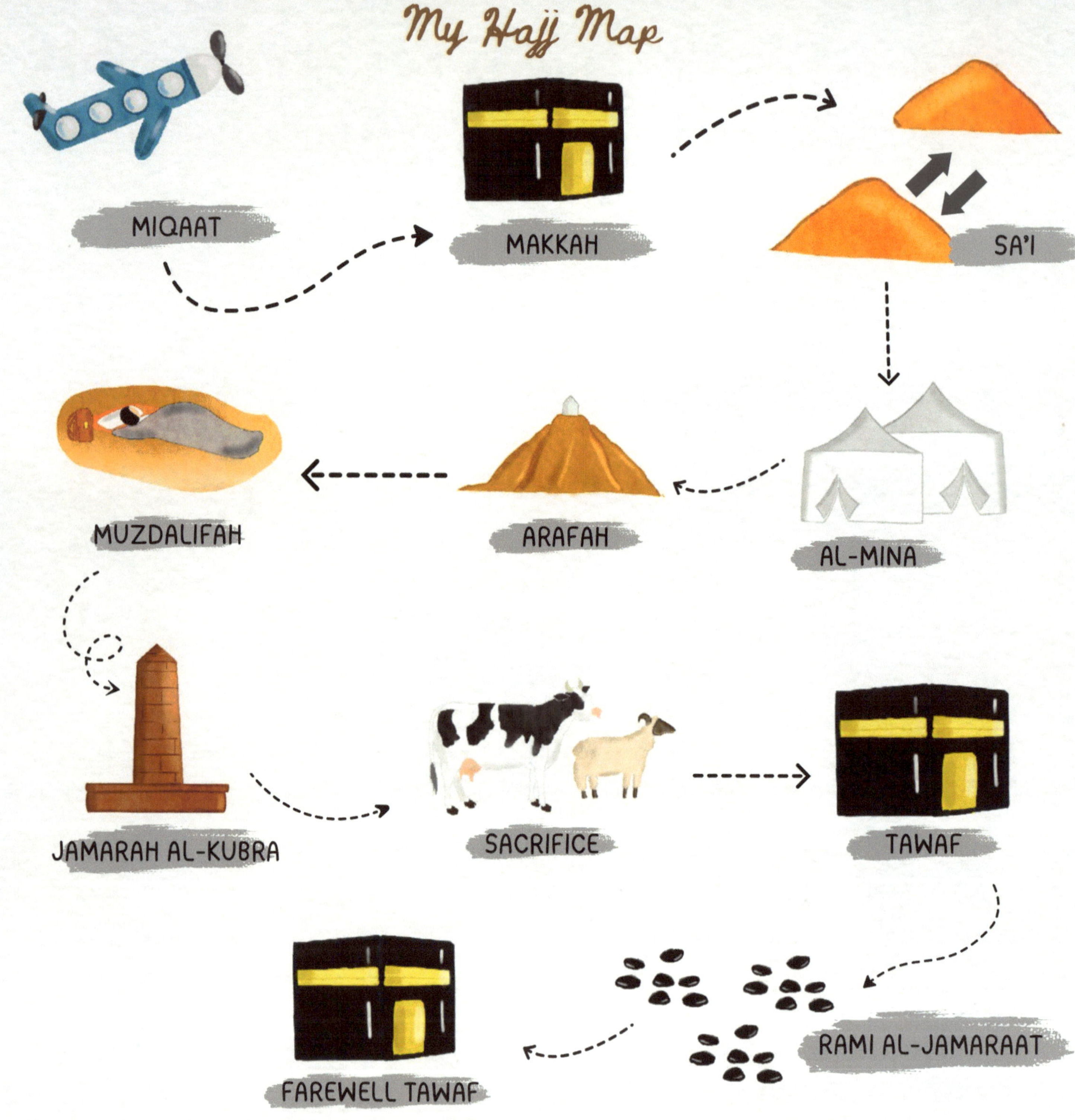